D0040981

MR. BOSTON

holiday
COCKTAILS

MR. BOSTON
holiday
COCKTAILS

Edited by Anthony Giglio and Jim Meehan
Photography by Ben Fink

WILEY
john wiley & sons, inc.

Published by John Wiley & Sons, Inc., Hoboken, New Jersey

Published simultaneously in Canada

For general information on our other products and services or for technical support, please contact our Customer Care Department within the United States at (800) 762-2974, outside the United States at (317) 572-3993 or fax (317) 572-4002.

Wiley also publishes its books in a variety of electronic formats. Some content that appears in print may not be available in electronic books. For more information about Wiley products, visit our web site at www.wiley.com.

Food and prop styling by Roy Finamore

Library of Congress Cataloging-in-Publication Data:

Giglio, Anthony.
  Mr. Boston holiday cocktails / edited by Anthony Giglio and Jim Meehan ; photography by Ben Fink.
      p. cm.
  Includes index.
  ISBN 978-0-470-18541-4 (cloth)
  1. Cocktails. 2. Entertaining. I. Meehan, Jim. II. Title.
  TX951.G476 2009
  641.8'74--dc22
                              2009001801

Printed in China

10 9 8 7 6 5 4 3 2 1

contents

Welcome!

You are holding in your hand the "Holiday Entertaining" edition of the definitive guide to mixing perfect drinks. *Mr. Boston Bartender's Guide* has been the official go-to manual of bartenders and spirits professionals since it was first published in 1935. It has been endorsed, consulted, and considered a basic tool for bartenders for decades. In fact, more than 11 million copies have been in print since it first appeared shortly after the repeal of Prohibition.

This book is the first of its kind for *Mr. Boston*: a guide written specifically with entertaining in mind. We'd like to think that this latest incarnation would have very much pleased Leo Cotton, the author of the very hard-to-find first edition of what was then called the *Old Mr. Boston Deluxe Official Bartenders Guide*, as he was known to be the life of any party he attended.

And speaking of parties, we've gathered 100 recipes for this edition from some of the best bartenders in the country that are guaranteed to please your guests at any gathering. We've categorized these recipes into five thematic chapters, each encompassing drinks that range from classics and riffs on classics to cutting edge and totally trendy.

We must admit that we encountered some interesting ingredients while consulting the most imaginative, inventive, and—yes, we're going to say it—brilliant bartenders in the country, including specialty spices, flavored syrups, and just-plain-funky concoctions (rose petal jam, anyone?). What we found, however, is that any dogged drinks maven can do a quick search on the Internet to find a recipe or retail source for just about anything these bartenders poured for us. Still, it's worth reminding our readers that some of the best cocktails ever created were those employing substitutes, plus a little imagination. Consider yourselves inspired.

Before you continue reading, however, please take a moment to think about the responsible use and serving of alcoholic drinks. The consumption of alcohol dates back many millennia, and in many cultures throughout the world is part of social rituals associated with significant occasions and celebrations. The majority of adults who choose to drink do not abuse alcohol and are aware that responsible drinking is key to their own enjoyment, health, and safety, as well as that of others, particularly when driving.

Finally, a word on the employment of fresh eggs in the nogs and flips in this book. While we are thrilled to see the recent rebirth of egg-based cocktails, we understand our readers' concerns over salmonella poisoning associated with raw eggs. While salmonella poisoning from eggs is relatively rare (see page 75), there are three alternatives to using raw eggs if you have any doubts about the freshness of your eggs: First, use a prepared mix such as Mr. Boston Egg Nog. Second, use pasteurized eggs, which can be found next to the regular eggs at good supermarkets. Third, if using regular eggs that have not been pasteurized, cook the egg mixture very slowly to 160°F, at which point the mixture thickens enough to coat a spoon, then refrigerate immediately. Also, if a recipe calls for folding beaten raw egg whites into a drink, you can use either pasteurized egg whites (separated by hand from the yolks) or prepackaged egg whites found in the supermarket, which have already been pasteurized. Hopefully, you'll feel inspired—and safe enough—to use eggs in one of the delicious recipes in this book.

So, congratulations! You're well on your way to creating cocktails that will enhance your holiday entertaining—and, hopefully, make the task easier. Let's raise a proverbial glass in honor of Mr. Boston as he was introduced in his 1935 debut:

> Sirs—May we now present to you Old Mr. Boston in permanent form. We know you are going to like him. He is a jolly fellow, one of those rare individuals, everlastingly young, a distinct personality and famous throughout the land for his sterling qualities and genuine good fellowship. His friends number in the millions those who are great and those who are near great even as you and I. He is jovial and ever ready to accept the difficult role of "Life of the Party," a sympathetic friend who may be relied upon in any emergency. Follow his advice and there will be many pleasant times in store for you.
>
> Gentlemen, Old Mr. Boston.

CONTRIBUTORS

Eric Alperin

Jeff Berry

Jacques Bezuidenhout

Jamie Boudreau

Tad Carducci

Jason Crawley

Alex Day

Bryan Dayton

Dale DeGroff

John Deragon

Phil Duff

Nate Dumas

Damon Dyer

John Gertsen

Jeff Grdnich

Chris Hannah

Charles Joly

Misty Kalkofen

Don Lee

Jeffery Lindenmuth

Ryan Magarian

Toby Maloney

Lynnette Marrero

Nate Matheson

Jim Meehan

Brian Miller

Jeffrey Morgenthaler

Christy Pope

Jonny Raglin

Gary Regan

Julie Reiner

Jon Santer

Audrey Saunders

Aisha Sharpe

Willy Shine

LeNell Smothers

Chad Solomon

Kelley Swenson

Marcos Tello

Todd Thrasher

Danny Valdez

Charles Vexenat

Charlotte Voisey

Phil Ward

Neyah White

David Wondrich

equipment

the right tools make mixing drinks easier, but some tasks simply can't be done without the right gizmo.

BOSTON SHAKER: Two-piece set comprised of a mixing glass and a slightly larger metal container that acts as a cover for the mixing glass for shaking cocktails. The mixing glass can be used alone for stirring drinks that aren't shaken.

BARSPOON: Long-handled, shallow spoon with a twisted handle, used for stirring drinks.

HAWTHORNE STRAINER: Perforated metal top for the metal half of a Boston shaker, held in place by a wire coil. Serves as a strainer.

JULEP STRAINER: Perforated, spoon-shaped strainer used in conjunction with a mixing glass.

COCKTAIL SHAKER: Metal pitcher with a tight-fitting lid, under which sits a strainer. While styles vary widely, the popular retrostyle pitcher has a handle as well as a spout that's sealed with a twist-off cap.

ELECTRIC BLENDER: Absolutely necessary to purée fruit and even crush ice for certain recipes.

CUTTING BOARD: Either wood or plastic, it is used to cut fruit for garnishes.

PARING KNIFE: Small, sharp knife to prepare fruit for garnishes.

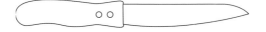

MUDDLER: Looks like a wooden pestle, the flat end of which is used to crush and combine ingredients in a serving glass or mixing glass.

GRATER: Useful for zesting fruit or grating nutmeg.

BOTTLE OPENER: Essential for opening bottles that aren't twist-off.

CHURCH KEY: Usually metal, it is pointed at one end to punch holes in the tops of cans, while the other end is used to open bottles.

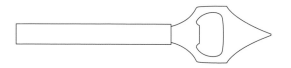

CORKSCREW: There are a myriad of styles from which to choose. Professionals use the "waiter's corkscrew," which looks like a penknife, the "screw-pull," or the "rabbit corkscrew." The "winged corkscrew," found in most homes, is considered easiest to use but often destroys the cork.

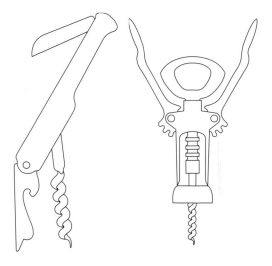

Waiter's corkscrew   Winged corkscrew

CITRUS REAMER: Essential for juicing fruit, it comes in two styles. The strainer bowl style has the pointed cone on top, or there is the wooden handle style with the cone attached, which must be used with a strainer.

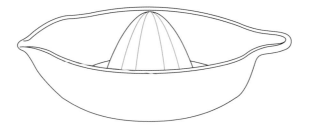

JIGGER: Essential for precise measuring, it typically has two cone-shaped metal cups conjoined at the narrow end—each side representing a quantity of ounces (quarter, half, whole, etc.), fractionalized by lines etched in the metal.

ICE BUCKET WITH SCOOP AND TONGS: A bar without ice is like a car without gas. Use the scoop—never the glass—to gather ice in a mixing glass or shaker and tongs to add single cubes to a prepared drink.

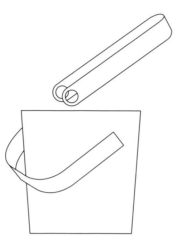

MISCELLANEOUS ACCOUTREMENTS: Sipsticks or stirrers, straws, cocktail napkins, coasters, and cocktail picks.

glassware

clean, polished glasses show off good drinks to great advantage. The best glasses should be thin-lipped, transparent, and sound off in high registers when "pinged." In practice, these glasses could be used to make the mixed drinks and cocktails found in this book:

COCKTAIL GLASS (ALSO KNOWN AS MARTINI GLASS): Typically 4 to 7 ounces, but lately much larger.

COLLINS GLASS: Tall and narrow, typically 8 to 12 ounces.

HIGHBALL GLASS: Shorter Collins glass, typically 8 to 10 ounces.

OLD-FASHIONED GLASS: Wide and squat, typically 6 to 8 ounces.

BRANDY SNIFTER: Balloon-shaped bowl with a short stem, typically 12 to 16 ounces.

Cocktail glass
(Martini glass)

Collins glass

Highball glass

Old-fashioned glass

Brandy snifter

CHAMPAGNE COUPE: Martini-style glass with rounded curves and flat bottom, typically 5 to 8 ounces.

CHAMPAGNE FLUTE: Long stem with a test-tube-like bowl to preserve the bubbles, typically 6 to 8 ounces.

IRISH COFFEE GLASS: a sturdy, heatproof glass mug with a short stem and stout base, typically 8 to 12 ounces.

RED WINE GLASS: Stem glass with large, round or tulip-shape bowl, typically 5 to 8 ounces—though sizes vary widely.

WHITE WINE GLASS: Stem glass with tulip-shape bowl, typically 5 to 8 ounces—though sizes vary widely.

Champagne coupe

Champagne flute

Irish coffee glass

Red wine glass

White wine glass

techniques

CHILLING GLASSWARE

Always chill before you fill—even your cocktail shaker—before mixing the drink. There are two ways to make a cocktail glass cold:

1. Put the glasses in the refrigerator or freezer a couple of hours before using them.

2. Fill the glasses with ice and water, stir, then discard when drink is ready.

FLAMING LIQUORS

The secret of setting brandy (or other high-alcohol spirits) aflame is first to warm it and its glass until almost hot. You can warm a glass by holding it by its stem above the flame or electric coil on your stove until the glass feels warm. (Avoid touching the glass to the flame or coil, which could char or crack it.)

Next, heat some brandy in a saucepan above the flame (or in a cooking pan). When the brandy is hot, ignite it with a match. If it's hot enough, it will flame instantly.

Pour the flaming liquid carefully into the other brandy you want flamed. If all the liquid is warm enough, it will ignite.

Warning: Flames can shoot high suddenly. Look up and be sure there's nothing "en route" that can ignite. That includes your hair. Have an open box of baking soda handy in case of accidents. Pour the baking soda over flames to extinguish them. Use pot holders to protect your hands from the hot glass, spoon, or pan.

FLOATING LIQUEURS

Creating a rainbow effect in a glass with different colored cordials requires a special pouring technique. Simply pour each liqueur slowly over an inverted teaspoon (rounded side up) into a glass: Start with the heaviest liqueur first. (Recipes will give proper order.) Pour slowly. The rounded surface of the spoon will spread each liqueur over the one beneath without mixing them. You can accomplish the same trick using a glass rod. Pour slowly down the rod.

CHOOSING FRUIT AND FRUIT JUICES

Whenever possible, use only fresh fruit. Wash the outside peel before using. Fruit can be cut in wedges or in slices. If slices are used, they should be cut about one-quarter inch thick and slit toward the center to fix the slice on the rim of the glass. Make sure garnishes are fresh and cold.

When mixing drinks containing fruit juices, always pour the liquor last. Squeeze and strain fruit juices just before using to ensure freshness and good taste. Avoid artificial, concentrated substitutes. When recipes call for a twist of lemon peel, rub a narrow strip or peel around the rim of the glass to deposit the oil on it. Then twist the peel so that the oil drops into the drink. Then drop in the peel. The lemon oil gives added character to the cocktail.

MUDDLING FRUIT AND HERBS

Muddling is a simple technique for releasing the essential oils in fruit and herbs, such as mint. You can buy a wooden muddler in a bar supply store; they typically range from six to ten inches long, flattened on one end (the muddling end) and rounded on the other (the handle). When muddling pulpy or fibrous fruit, you might want to pass the liquid through a tea strainer before serving.

RIMMING A GLASS

This technique separates the pros from the amateurs. Into a saucer or a small bowl pour kosher salt—never use iodized salt—or sugar, depending on the drink. Using a wedge of fresh lemon or lime, carefully wet only the outside rim of the cocktail glass. Then, holding the glass sideways, dab the rim into the salt while slowly turning the glass, until the entire rim is covered. Finally, hold the glass and tap the glass gently against your free hand to knock off any excess salt. The effect is a delicately salted rim that looks almost frosted.

ROLLING DRINKS

To prevent drinks that call for thick juices or fruit purées from foaming, roll them instead of shaking. Rolling is the act of pouring the drink—a Bloody Mary, for example—back and forth between two shaker glasses. After rolling the drink a half-dozen times, it should be completely incorporated and ready to be strained.

SHAKING

As a rule of thumb, shake any drink made with juices, eggs, or cream.

assemble

Assemble the ingredients in the glass part of the Boston shaker, adding the fresh juice first before the ice, then the dashes, modifiers, and the base spirit, followed by the ice.

seal

Place the metal half of the Boston shaker over the glass while it's sitting on the bar. Holding the glass firmly, clap the upturned end of the metal half twice with the heel of your free hand to form a seal. (To test the seal, lift the shaker by the metal top slightly off the bar to see if it holds; if not, do it again or replace one of the parts.)

flip, then shake

Turn the conjoined shakers over so that the glass is on top and the metal half rests on the bar. Grasp the shakers with the metal half sitting securely in the palm of one hand and the other hand wrapped securely over the top of the glass half, then shake hard with the glass half of the set on top. (In case the seal breaks, the liquid stays in the bigger metal half.) Shake vigorously.

break it up

After shaking, clasp one hand around the equator of the conjoined shakers and then, using the heel of your other hand, hit the top rim of the metal shaker bluntly to break the seal. If it doesn't work the first time, rotate the shakers slightly and try again.

strain and pour

If you're the least bit theatrical, this is the time for it. Just remember: Always use the Hawthorne strainer (springform) with the metal part of the set and the Julep strainer (holes) with the glass half. (See Straining, below.)

STIRRING

While you can prepare stirred drinks like Negronis, Martinis, and Manhattans in any number of vessels, the glass part of the Boston shaker is considered best. After you've assembled your liquids and ice, hold the barspoon by the twisted shaft, between your thumb and first two fingers. Plunge the spoon end into the mixing glass and begin twirling the spoon back and forth between your fingers. Do this for at least 15 seconds to completely chill the cocktail, while also allowing sufficient time for the ice to melt.

straining from the metal shaker

Place the Hawthorne strainer on top, then put your forefinger and middle finger on top of the strainer while grabbing the shaker with your thumb, ring, and pinky fingers. Hold the shaker tightly and strain slowly at first to avoid splashing out of the glass. As the pour slows toward the last ounce, draw your hand up high over the middle of the cocktail glass, emptying the last of the liquid with a snap of the shaker.

straining from the glass shaker

Place the Julep strainer over the top of the glass with the concave side facing up. Grab the glass toward the top with your thumb and three fingers, and then curl your forefinger over the handle of the strainer, holding it firmly in place. Strain following the directions above.

OPENING CHAMPAGNE OR SPARKLING WINE

When the bottle is well chilled, wrap it in a clean towel and undo the wire around the cork, holding the cork down with one hand while loosening the wire with the other—never letting go of the cork. Pointing the bottle away from people and priceless objects, grasp the bottle by the indentation on the bottom, and leveraging the pressure between both hands, slowly turn the bottle (not the cork!) until the cork comes free with a gentle pop. Pour slowly into the center of the glass.

OPENING WINE

Cut the seal neatly around the neck with a sharp knife just below the top. Peel off, exposing the cork. Wipe off the cork and bottle lip. Insert the corkscrew and turn until the corkscrew is completely inside the cork. With a steady pull, remove the cork. If the cork crumbles or breaks, pour the wine through a tea strainer into another container for serving. The host or hostess should taste the wine to check its quality before offering it to guests.

how many drinks per bottle

COCKTAILS, MIXED DRINKS

1.5-ounce liquor servings

BOTTLES	1	2	4	6	8	10	12
750-ml	16	33	67	101	135	169	203
1.5-liter	39	78	157	236	315	394	473

seasonal
SIPPERS

The effort it takes to incorporate seasonal fresh fruits in your cocktails is justly rewarded within seconds of the very first taste of the cocktail bearing—literally—the fruits of your labor. Whether you're simply muddling kumquats or painstakingly seeding pomegranates to make fresh grenadine syrup (an admittedly laborious endeavor—see "Grenadine Grit," page 80), the results always far outweigh the task, imbuing your drinks with flavor and intensity that can only come from fresh, unprocessed fruit. The following recipes feature, for the most part, fruits that we're more likely to find during the holiday months, but thanks to global shipping, you might be able to find many of these ingredients year-round. As we strive to become ever more conscious of the purity and freshness of the ingredients in our cocktails, we'd like to suggest at least trying to procure ingredients grown locally, if possible.

basil 8

basil 8

3 BASIL LEAVES

5 WHITE GRAPES, PLUS 1 FOR GARNISH

1¹/₂ OZ. VODKA

³/₄ OZ. FRESH LIME JUICE

1 OZ. SIMPLE SYRUP

1 DASH OF ANGOSTURA BITTERS

GINGER ALE

GARNISH: BASIL SPRIG

muddle the basil leaves and 5 grapes in a Collins glass. Top with ice cubes and add the rest of the ingredients, topping off with ginger ale. Garnish with the basil sprig and 1 white grape.

{trade secret}

SWITCH UP YOUR SWEETENER

Simple syrup provides the essential needed balance—but no flavor—in drinks mixed with fresh citrus. When the mercury drops, make rich simple syrup with 2 parts Demerara sugar to 1 part water, or use maple syrup. Use half the amount of regular simple syrup called for in the recipe to enrich brown spirit-based drinks balanced with aromatic bitters. For white spirit-based drinks, try using honey or agave syrup (1 part each sweetener and hot water, stirred until dissolved) to add complexity and body. Pomegranates can be pressed and sweetened into grenadine, or fresh juice can be purchased and sweetened with superfine sugar. Almond and orange flower water-based orgeat provides a bright, nutty accent that works especially well in rum- and brandy-based cocktails.

big spender

1½ OZ. AÑEJO TEQUILA

1 OZ. CLÉMENT CRÉOLE SHRUBB

¾ OZ. FRESH BLOOD ORANGE JUICE

ROSÉ CHAMPAGNE

GARNISH: FLAMED ORANGE TWIST (SEE PAGE 91)

combine the first three ingredients in a mixing glass and add ice cubes. Stir and strain into a chilled Champagne flute. Top off with rosé Champagne. Garnish with the flamed orange twist.

{trade secret}

FREESTYLE FRUITS

Just because the recipes in this book are geared toward the winter holiday months—with their emphasis on seasonal ingredients—doesn't mean you can't make them any time of year, especially if you keep to the "freshest is best" ideal when making any cocktail, any time. For instance, when fresh blueberries, cranberries, or huckleberries go out of season, work with whichever berries you can find in the market. The same goes for citrus fruits that change seasonally, such as blood oranges; if all you can find are, say, Valencia oranges, why not squeeze them and add a splash of grenadine to add some of that hallmark blood orange color and sweet-and-tart flavor?

bitter end

¾ OZ. STRAIGHT RYE WHISKEY

¾ OZ. FRESH LEMON JUICE

¾ OZ. LICOR 43

¾ OZ. AMARO

1 LARGE EGG WHITE

SODA WATER

GARNISH: FRESHLY GRATED NUTMEG

combine the first five ingredients in a cocktail shaker and shake without ice cubes. Add ice cubes, shake, and strain into a highball glass. Top off with a splash of soda water. Garnish with grated nutmeg.

bitter end no. 2

1 OZ. CAMPARI

¼ OZ. YELLOW CHARTREUSE

2 OZ. FRESH BLOOD ORANGE JUICE

CHAMPAGNE

combine the first three ingredients in a cocktail shaker, add ice cubes, and shake thoroughly. Strain into a chilled Champagne flute. Top off with Champagne.

bitterly dark

1 OZ. FRESH BLOOD ORANGE JUICE

1½ OZ. AGED RUM

1 OZ. AMARO

¼ OZ. CRÈME DE CASSIS

GARNISH: BLOOD ORANGE WHEEL

combine all of the ingredients in a cocktail shaker, add ice cubes, and shake thoroughly. Strain into a chilled cocktail glass. Garnish with the blood orange wheel.

blood-and-sand

¾ OZ. FRESH ORANGE JUICE

1½ OZ. SCOTCH WHISKY

¾ OZ. CHERRY-FLAVORED BRANDY

¾ OZ. SWEET VERMOUTH

combine all of the ingredients in a cocktail shaker, add ice cubes, and shake thoroughly. Strain into a chilled cocktail glass.

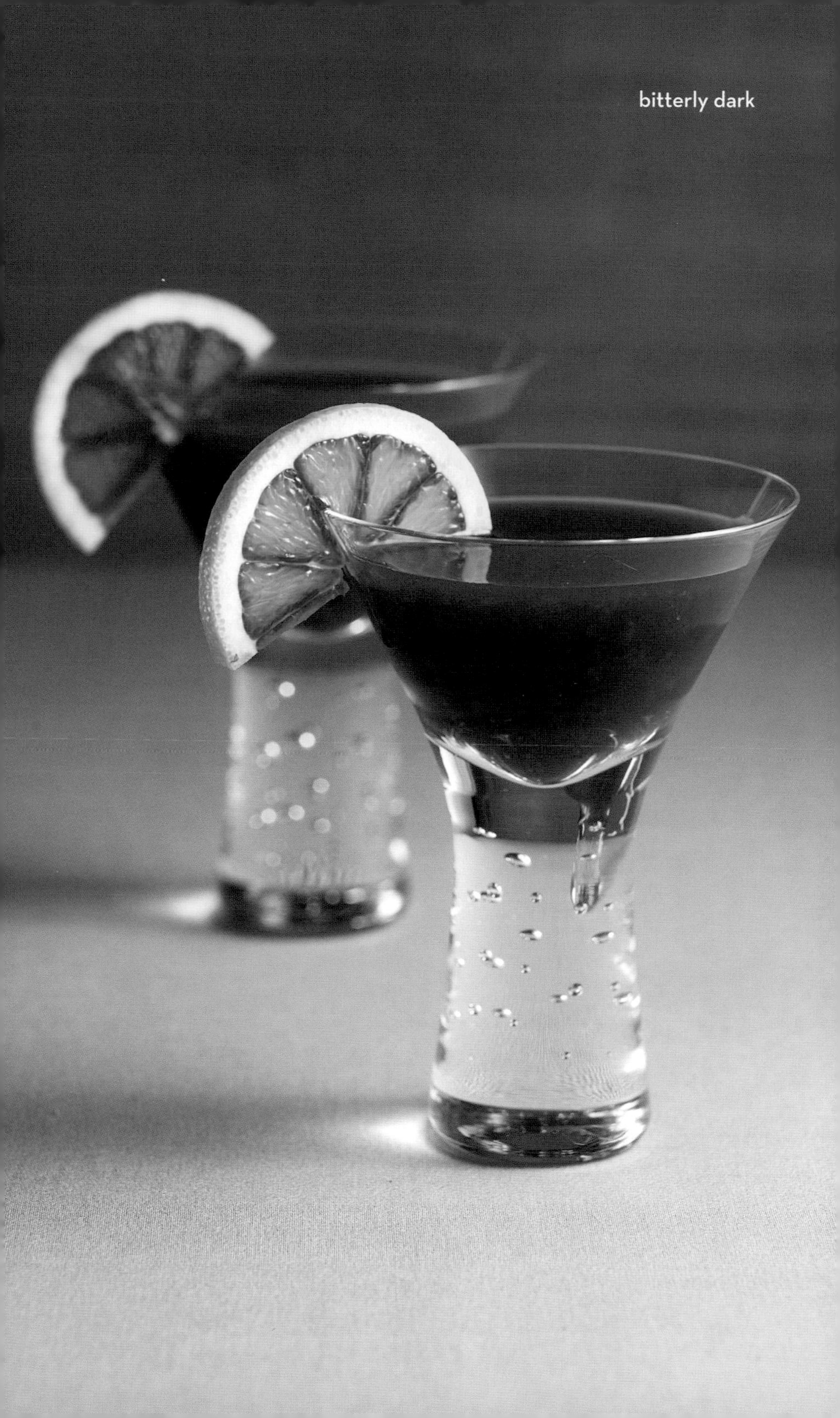
bitterly dark

grand porto

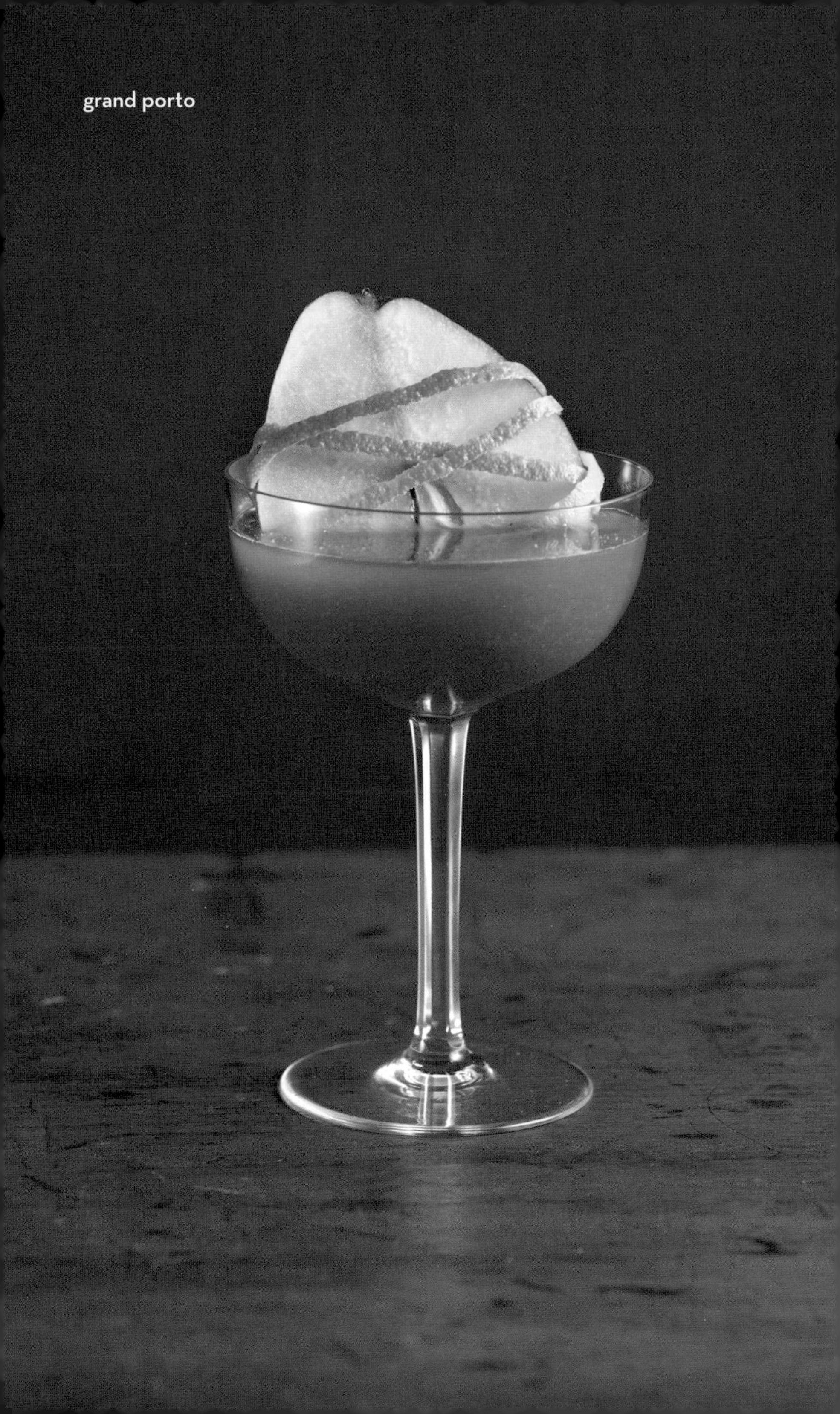

grand porto

1 OZ. TAWNY PORT

3/4 OZ. ORANGE CURAÇAO

3/4 OZ. PEAR PURÉE

1/4 OZ. FRESH LEMON JUICE

GARNISH: GREEN PEAR SLICE WRAPPED IN AN ORANGE TWIST

combine all of the ingredients in a cocktail shaker, add ice cubes, and shake thoroughly. Strain into a chilled Champagne coupe. Garnish with the pear slice.

{trade secret}

GETTING REAL

Before you decide what drinks to serve at your party, think about local fruits or vegetables that are in season at your nearby grocery or farmers' market, and try to incorporate them into the party. In the dead of winter, there's still a variety of apples and pears available, and especially great citrus in the form of clementines and blood oranges. And dried fruits such as figs, raisins, dates, and tamarind work particularly well in winter spirit infusions.

jack rose

1½ OZ. APPLE BRANDY

½ OZ. FRESH LEMON JUICE

1 TSP. GRENADINE SYRUP (SEE PAGE 80)

combine all of the ingredients in a cocktail shaker, add ice cubes, and shake thoroughly. Strain into a chilled cocktail glass.

jerry's ruin

2 OZ. SPICED RUM

½ OZ. CINNAMON SYRUP

½ OZ. FRESH LIME JUICE

1 OZ. CRANBERRY JUICE COCKTAIL

2 DASHES OF ANGOSTURA BITTERS

combine all of the ingredients in a cocktail shaker, add ice cubes, and shake thoroughly. Strain into a chilled Champagne coupe.

juniper breeze

2 OZ. GIN

2 OZ. CRANBERRY JUICE COCKTAIL

1 OZ. FRESH GRAPEFRUIT JUICE

GARNISH: GRAPEFRUIT HALF-WHEEL

fill a Collins glass with ice cubes. Add the gin and juices. Garnish with the grapefruit half-wheel.

kin kan sour

5 KUMQUATS

½ OZ. SIMPLE SYRUP

2 OZ. GIN

¼ OZ. ELDERFLOWER LIQUEUR

muddle the kumquats and simple syrup in a cocktail shaker. Add the gin and liqueur and top with ice cubes. Shake thoroughly and strain into a chilled Champagne coupe.

lancaster-on-hudson

2 OZ. STRAIGHT BOURBON WHISKEY

1 BARSPOON OF APPLE BUTTER

3/4 OZ. MAPLE SYRUP

1 OZ. FRESH LEMON JUICE

2 DASHES OF ABSINTHE

GARNISH: RED APPLE SLICE

combine all of the ingredients in a cocktail shaker, add ice cubes, and shake thoroughly. Strain into an old-fashioned glass filled with ice cubes. Garnish with the apple slice.

lillypad

1 1/2 OZ. BLANCO TEQUILA

1/2 OZ. LILLET BLANC

1/2 OZ. LILLET ROUGE

1 1/2 OZ. APPLE JUICE

1/4 OZ. AGAVE NECTAR

3/4 OZ. LIME JUICE

GARNISH: BLOOD ORANGE WHEEL

combine all of the ingredients in a cocktail shaker, add ice cubes, and shake thoroughly. Strain into a chilled cocktail glass. Garnish with the blood orange wheel.

lime and white
chocolate swizzle

lime and white chocolate swizzle

1½ OZ. AGED RUM

1 OZ. FRESH LIME JUICE

½ OZ. WHITE CRÈME DE CACAO

½ OZ. VANILLA SYRUP

1 DASH OF ANGOSTURA BITTERS

GARNISH: PINEAPPLE LEAF

fill a collins glass with crushed ice and add the ingredients in order. Swizzle for 10 seconds. Top with more crushed ice. Garnish with the pineapple leaf.

mad dog cocktail

2 OZ. SMOKY SINGLE MALT SCOTCH WHISKY

1 OZ. GALLIANO

¾ OZ. FRESH LEMON JUICE

2 DASHES OF PASTIS

GARNISH: LEMON TWIST

combine all of the ingredients in a cocktail shaker, add ice cubes, and shake thoroughly. Strain into a chilled Champagne coupe. Garnish with the lemon twist.

made in the shade

1¹/₂ OZ. VODKA

1¹/₂ OZ. BREWED ESPRESSO

¹/₂ OZ. VELVET FALERNUM

¹/₂ OZ. SWEETENED CONDENSED MILK

1 DASH OF PEACH BITTERS

GARNISH: 3 COFFEE BEANS

combine all of the ingredients in a cocktail shaker, add ice cubes, and shake thoroughly. Strain into a chilled Champagne coupe. Garnish with the coffee beans.

pink lady

1¹/₂ OZ. GIN

¹/₂ OZ. APPLEJACK

³/₄ OZ. FRESH LEMON JUICE

¹/₄ OZ. GRENADINE SYRUP (SEE PAGE 80)

1 LARGE EGG WHITE

combine all of the ingredients in a cocktail shaker and shake without ice cubes. Add ice cubes, shake thoroughly, and strain into a chilled cocktail glass.

pink lady

sunset at gowanus

2 OZ. AGED RUM

³/₄ OZ. LIME JUICE

¹/₂ OZ. MAPLE SYRUP

¹/₄ OZ. APPLE BRANDY

¹/₄ OZ. YELLOW CHARTREUSE

combine all of the ingredients in a cocktail shaker, add ice cubes, and shake thoroughly. Strain into a chilled cocktail glass.

sweet and vicious

1 TSP. MAPLE SYRUP

2 OZ. STRAIGHT RYE WHISKEY

¹/₂ OZ. DRY VERMOUTH

¹/₂ OZ. AMARO

1 THIN FUJI APPLE SLICE PLUS, 1 FOR GARNISH

add 1 apple slice and the maple syrup to a mixing glass and muddle. Add all of the remaining ingredients and ice cubes. Stir and strain into a chilled cocktail glass. Garnish with the remaining apple slice.

tommy's cocktail

1½ OZ. VANILLA-FLAVORED RUM

½ OZ. LICOR 43

2 OZ. POMEGRANATE JUICE

½ OZ. SIMPLE SYRUP

¼ OZ. FRESH ORANGE JUICE

1 LARGE EGG WHITE

GARNISH: POMEGRANATE MOLASSES

combine all of the ingredients in a cocktail shaker and shake without ice cubes. Add ice cubes, shake thoroughly, and strain into a chilled Champagne coupe. Garnish with a few drops of pomegranate molasses over the froth.

{trade secret}

PRINT A RECIPE CARD

If your drink is well received (and why shouldn't it be!), your guests may very well ask you for the recipe. Be prepared by printing up recipe cards that include the ingredients you used to make the drink, where you purchased them—especially if they're tough to find—and any helpful background information, such as the book you sourced the recipe from or the occasion for which it was served.

xochitl

**TO RIM THE GLASS: FINE SALT, SUGAR, GROUND CINNAMON, LIME
    WEDGE**

1¹/₂ OZ. REPOSADO TEQUILA

³/₄ OZ. BELLE DE BRILLET

1 OZ. PEAR PURÉE

¹/₂ OZ. FRESH LIME JUICE

GARNISH: PEAR SLICE

combine equal parts salt, sugar, and ground cinnamon. Moisten
the edge of a Champagne coupe with the lime wedge and dip in the
mixture. Combine the tequila, Belle de Brillet, pear purée, and lime
juice in a cocktail shaker, add ice cubes, and shake thoroughly. Strain
into the Champagne coupe. Garnish with the pear slice.

{trade secret}

SET BOUNDARIES

Face it—we all have friends and
family members who, shall we
say, know how to imbibe with
vigor, often to excess. There-
fore, it's best to include the
duration of a party on invita-
tions, and then stock your bar
with only what is needed for
the event. Sure, it's uncomfort-
able to turn the lights out on
your friends—or raise the dim-
mer wattage for "last call!"—so
be courteous about wrapping
things up, then suggest where
to relocate the party, or, better
yet, convince them to go home.

perfect
PUNCHES

The origin of punch makes for great discourse and debate while standing around the proverbial punch bowl. Regardless of whether it takes its name from the Hindustani *panch* (which means "five" and is purported to be the number of ingredients needed to make one) or is derived from *puncheon* (an old English wine cask that, once cut open, made one heck of a big punch bowl), the common denominator is that it's a delicious concoction served in large quantities to make many people happy simultaneously.

In all seriousness, there is no single better drink idea for a host to consider when he or she intends to enjoy guests' company without the demanding distraction of playing bartender. As for what constitutes a proper punch, the sky's the limit. Any cocktail recipe can be multiplied to fit in a punch bowl, but the essential key for any *cold* punch—which makes up the majority of the recipes in this chapter—is ice, a very big block of it or a handmade mold. Unless otherwise stated, these recipes yield approximately twelve 4- to 5-ounce servings.

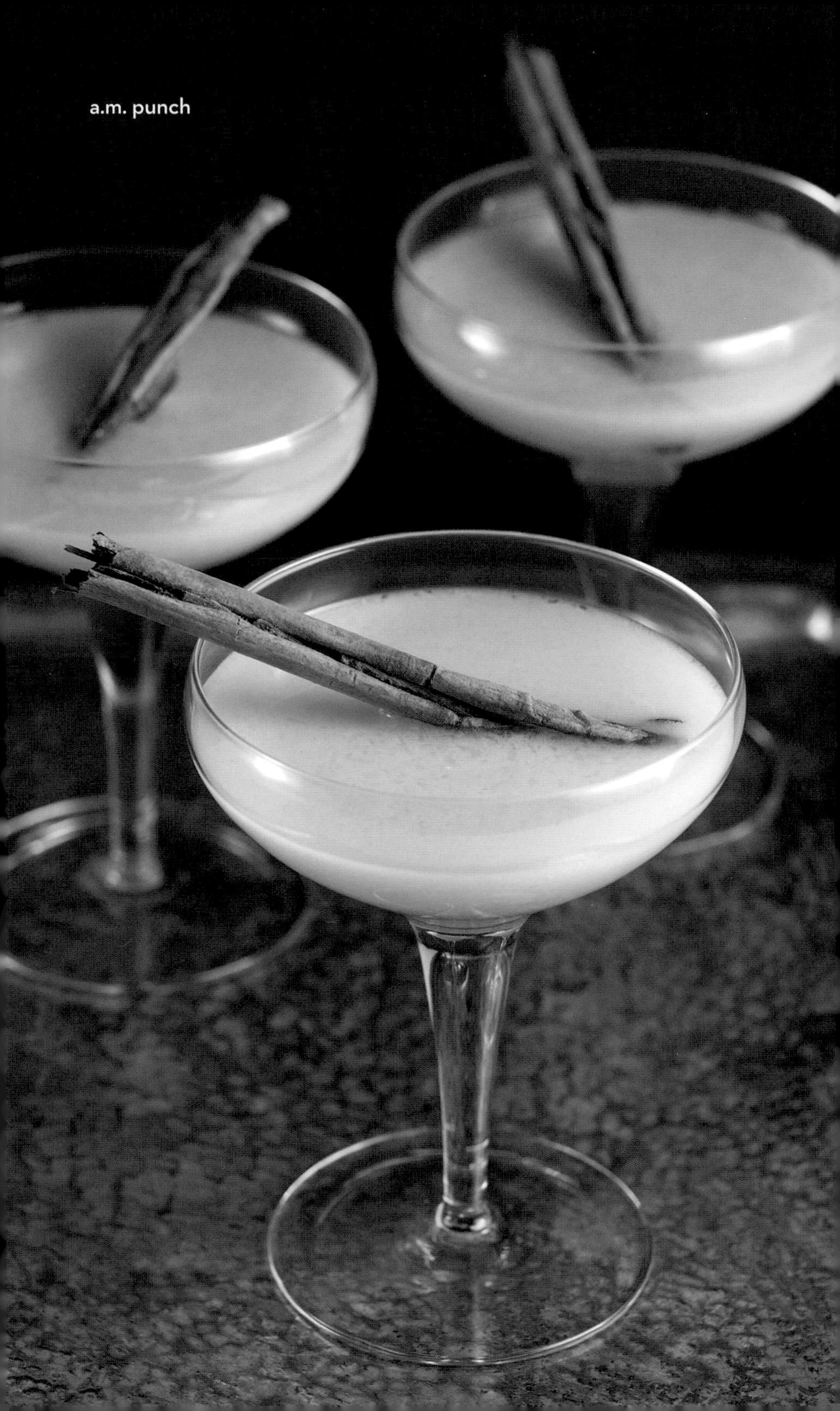
a.m. punch

a.m. punch

10 OZ. AÑEJO TEQUILA

10 OZ. APPLE BRANDY

5 OZ. ELDERFLOWER LIQUEUR

10 OZ. FRESH LEMON JUICE

5 OZ. ORGEAT

8 OZ. CHILLED SPARKLING APPLE CIDER

GARNISH: CINNAMON STICKS

combine all of the ingredients in a punch bowl and add a large ice mold or block of ice. Ladle into chilled Champagne coupes. Garnish each with a cinnamon stick.

appeasement punch

6 OZ. AGAVE NECTAR

6 OZ. FRESHLY BREWED OOLONG TEA

20 OZ. APPLE BRANDY

8 OZ. LILLET BLANC

2 OZ. ALLSPICE LIQUEUR (ALSO KNOWN AS PIMENTO DRAM)

6 OZ. FRESH LEMON JUICE

GARNISH: ORANGE TWISTS

combine the agave nectar and tea and stir thoroughly. Chill. Combine the rest of the ingredients in a punch bowl and stir in the agave-tea mixture. Add a large ice mold or block of ice. Ladle into chilled punch glasses filled with ice cubes. Garnish each with an orange twist.

bombay punch

2 OZ. SIMPLE SYRUP

5 OZ. FRESH LEMON JUICE

6$^1/_2$ OZ. BRANDY

6$^1/_2$ OZ. DRY SHERRY

$^3/_4$ OZ. MARASCHINO LIQUEUR

$^3/_4$ OZ. TRIPLE SEC

ONE 750-ML BOTTLE CHAMPAGNE, CHILLED

13 OZ. CHILLED SODA WATER

GARNISH: CUT SEASONAL FRUITS, PEELED IF NECESSARY

place a large ice mold or block of ice in a punch bowl and pour the ingredients over it. Stir thoroughly. Ladle into chilled punch glasses. Garnish with seasonal fruits.

{trade secret}

THE FIZZY FOUNDATION

Consider the other ingredients in a punch before deciding which wine (sparkling or otherwise), beer, or soda is the best complement. Champagne usually does the trick, but cava and prosecco work well when you're on a budget. Always use fresh bottles of beer or soda when you're mixing drinks and look for brands made with all natural ingredients. Remember, a chain is only as strong as its weakest link.

brighton punch

6 OZ. STRAIGHT BOURBON WHISKEY

6 OZ. BRANDY

6 OZ. BÉNÉDICTINE

12 OZ. FRESH ORANGE JUICE

6 OZ. FRESH LEMON JUICE

ONE 18-OZ. BOTTLE SODA WATER, CHILLED

GARNISH: ORANGE AND LEMON WHEELS

combine the first five ingredients in a punch bowl and stir thoroughly. Add a large ice mold or block of ice and the soda water. Stir gently. Ladle into chilled punch glasses. Garnish each with orange and lemon wheels.

bum's rush

18 OZ. BLANCO TEQUILA

9 OZ. TRIPLE SEC

9 OZ. HONEY LIQUEUR

12 OZ. FRESH LIME JUICE

12 OZ. APPLE CIDER

GARNISH: LIME WEDGES

combine all of the ingredients in a punch bowl and stir thoroughly. Add a large ice mold or block of ice. Ladle into chilled punch glasses. Garnish each with a lime wedge.

claret cup

2 OZ. SIMPLE SYRUP

12 OZ. CHILLED SODA WATER

4 OZ. TRIPLE SEC

8 OZ. BRANDY

ONE 750-ML BOTTLE RED BORDEAUX WINE, CHILLED

SEASONAL FRUIT SUCH AS APPLES, PEARS, BERRIES, CITRUS, IN PIECES, PEELED PER PREFERENCE

SKIN OF 1 MEDIUM CUCUMBER, IN STRIPS

GARNISH: MINT SPRIGS

combine all of the ingredients in a punch bowl and stir thoroughly. Add a large ice mold or block of ice. Ladle into chilled wine glasses. Garnish each with a mint sprig.

dementia pugilistica

12 OZ. COGNAC

2 OZ. MARASCHINO LIQUEUR

2 OZ. ELDERFLOWER LIQUEUR

TWO 750-ML BOTTLES ROSÉ CHAMPAGNE, CHILLED

6 DASHES OF ANGOSTURA BITTERS

10 DASHES OF PEACH BITTERS

GARNISH: BLOOD ORANGE WHEELS

combine all of the ingredients in a punch bowl and stir gently. Add a large ice mold or block of ice. Ladle into chilled Champagne coupes. Garnish each with a blood orange wheel.

claret cup

duck blind punch

duck blind punch

36 OZ. APPLE CIDER

6 OZ. FRESH ORANGE JUICE

4 EARL GREY TEA BAGS

13 OZ. STRAIGHT RYE WHISKEY

13 OZ. AGED RUM

GARNISH: FRESHLY GRATED NUTMEG

fill a punch bowl with hot water. Combine the cider and orange juice in a saucepan. Bring to a boil over high heat. Remove the saucepan from the heat and add the tea bags. Allow to steep for 3 minutes. Remove and discard the tea bags. Carefully discard the hot water from the punch bowl and pour in the hot mixture. Stir in the rye and rum. Ladle into preheated tea cups. Garnish each with nutmeg.

extended roman holiday punch

16 OZ. COGNAC

8 OZ. ST. GERMAIN ELDERFLOWER LIQUEUR

6 OZ. RAMAZOTTI AMARO

6 OZ. LEMON JUICE

12 OZ. SODA WATER

GARNISH: ORANGE SLICES

add all of the ingredients except the soda water to a large punch bowl and store in the fridge until you're ready to serve. For service: Add the soda water and a large block of ice. Serve in chilled highball glasses. Garnish each with an orange slice.

flying grandma

18 OZ. CITRUS VODKA

6 OZ. GRAND MARNIER

9 OZ. FRESH GRAPEFRUIT JUICE

60 MINT LEAVES (ABOUT 10 SPRIGS)

ONE 750-ML BOTTLE MOSCATO D'ASTI, CHILLED

GARNISH: GRAPEFRUIT TWISTS

combine the vodka, Grand Marnier, grapefruit juice, and mint in a large pitcher. Refrigerate for at least 30 minutes. Strain through a fine-mesh sieve into a punch bowl. Add a large ice mold or block of ice and the Moscato d'Asti and stir thoroughly. Ladle into chilled Champagne coupes. Garnish each with a grapefruit twist.

flying grandma

gantt's tomb

12 OZ. DARK RUM

12 OZ. STRAIGHT RYE WHISKEY

6 OZ. OVERPROOF WHITE RUM

9 OZ. FRESH PINEAPPLE JUICE

7 OZ. FRESH LEMON JUICE

6 OZ. FRESH ORANGE JUICE

6 OZ. SIMPLE SYRUP

2 OZ. ALLSPICE LIQUEUR (ALSO KNOWN AS PIMENTO DRAM)

GARNISH: FRESH MINT LEAVES

combine all of the ingredients in a punch bowl and stir thoroughly. Add a large ice mold or block of ice. Ladle into chilled punch glasses. Garnish each with a mint leaf.

{trade secret}

ICE, ICE, BABY!

In order to keep punch cold throughout a party without overdiluting it with conventional ice cubes, it's best to freeze a large block that fits neatly in the center of the punch bowl. A Tupperware bowl or silicone bread mold works perfectly, but feel free to improvise. Garnishes, syrups, or tea may be frozen into the block if you're feeling creative. For clear ice, pour warm water into the mold before placing in the freezer.

la cola nostra

14 OZ. AGED RUM

8 OZ. AMARO

6 OZ. FRESH LIME JUICE

4 OZ. SIMPLE SYRUP

2 OZ. ALLSPICE LIQUEUR (ALSO KNOWN AS PIMENTO DRAM)

ONE 750-ML BOTTLE CHAMPAGNE, CHILLED

GARNISH: FRESHLY GRATED NUTMEG

combine all of the ingredients in a punch bowl and stir gently. Add a large ice mold or block of ice. Ladle into chilled Champagne coupes. Garnish each with nutmeg.

last orders

14 OZ. AQUAVIT

4 OZ. FRANGELICO

6 OZ. BÉNÉDICTINE

TWO 12-OZ. BOTTLES PORTER OR STOUT

GARNISH: ORANGE TWISTS

combine all of the ingredients in a punch bowl and stir gently. Add a large ice mold or block of ice. Ladle into chilled punch glasses filled with cracked ice. Garnish each with an orange twist.

maxwell's return

3 TBSP. FRESH ROSEMARY LEAVES

6 OZ. SIMPLE SYRUP

24 OZ. GIN

12 OZ. FRESH PINEAPPLE JUICE

6 OZ. FRESH LIME JUICE

3 OZ. GREEN CHARTREUSE

GARNISH: ROSEMARY SPRIGS

muddle the rosemary leaves with the simple syrup in a pitcher. Strain through a fine-mesh sieve into a punch bowl. Add the rest of the ingredients and a large ice mold or block of ice and stir thoroughly. Ladle into chilled punch glasses. Garnish each with a rosemary sprig.

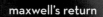

mill yard punch

16 OZ. APPLE BRANDY

6 OZ. AGED MARTINIQUE RUM

4 OZ. ORANGE CURAÇAO

1 OZ. OVERPROOF WHITE RUM

6 OZ. FRESH LEMON JUICE

3 OZ. SIMPLE SYRUP

6 OZ. BREWED CHAMOMILE TEA, CHILLED

6 OZ. APPLE CIDER

GARNISH: LEMON TWISTS

combine all of the ingredients in a punch bowl and stir thoroughly. Add a large ice mold or block of ice. Ladle into chilled punch glasses filled with cracked ice. Garnish each with a lemon twist.

prince of wales

Serves 8

9 OZ. SERCIAL MADEIRA

9 OZ. BRANDY

3 OZ. TRIPLE SEC

12 DASHES OF ANGOSTURA BITTERS

1/2 OF A 750-ML BOTTLE CHAMPAGNE

GARNISH: ORANGE TWISTS

combine the first four ingredients in a punch bowl and stir thoroughly. Add a large ice mold or block of ice. Ladle into chilled Champagne coupes and top off with Champagne. Garnish each with an orange twist.

rosé the riveter

12 OZ. GIN

1¹/₂ OZ. GRENADINE

¹/₂ OZ. HONEY SYRUP (SEE PAGE 3)

ONE 750-ML BOTTLE DRY ROSÉ WINE

8 OZ. SODA WATER

GARNISH: LIMES WHEELS

combine all of the ingredients in a punch bowl and stir gently. Add a large ice mold or block of ice. Ladle into chilled punch glasses filled with cracked ice. Garnish each with a lime wheel.

spiced winter punch

12 OZ. SPICED RUM

4 OZ. NAVAN VANILLA COGNAC

12 OZ. APPLE CIDER

4 OZ. MAPLE SYRUP

4 OZ. FRESH LEMON JUICE

ONE 12-OZ. BOTTLE JAMAICAN GINGER BEER

18 DASHES OF ANGOSTURA BITTERS

GARNISH: FRESHLY GRATED NUTMEG

combine all of the ingredients in a punch bowl and stir gently. Add a large ice mold or block of ice. Ladle into chilled punch glasses. Garnish each with nutmeg.

spice trader's tipple

14 OZ. AGED RUM

6 OZ. COGNAC

3 OZ. RUBY PORT

3 OZ. ORANGE CURAÇAO

6 OZ. FRESH LIME JUICE

4 OZ. SIMPLE SYRUP

ONE 12-OZ. BOTTLE JAMAICAN GINGER BEER

GARNISH: FRESHLY GRATED NUTMEG

combine all of the ingredients in a punch bowl and stir gently. Add a large ice mold or block of ice. Ladle into chilled punch glasses filled with cracked ice. Garnish each with nutmeg.

stone wall

6 TBSP. PEELED, CHOPPED FRESH GINGER

9 OZ. RICH SIMPLE SYRUP (SEE PAGE 3)

18 OZ. APPLE CIDER

18 OZ. AMBER RUM

18 OZ. JAMAICAN GINGER BEER (1½ BOTTLES)

GARNISHES: GREEN APPLE SLICES

muddle the ginger with the syrup in a pitcher. Strain through a fine-mesh sieve into a punch bowl. Add the cider, rum, and a large ice mold or block of ice. Stir thoroughly and ladle into chilled punch glasses. Top off with ginger beer and garnish each with an apple slice.

stone wall

sugared plum punch

10 OZ. PLUM BRANDY

7 OZ. CRÈME DE MÛRE

ONE 750-ML BOTTLE CHAMPAGNE

10 OZ. FRESH LEMON JUICE

3 OZ. SIMPLE SYRUP

GARNISH: LEMON TWISTS

combine all of the ingredients in a punch bowl and stir gently. Add a large ice mold or block of ice. Ladle into chilled Champagne coupes. Garnish each with a lemon twist.

winter night punch

12 OZ. COGNAC

10 OZ. TAWNY PORT

8 DASHES OF ANGOSTURA BITTERS

2 OZ. GRADE B MAPLE SYRUP

24 OZ. HOT WATER

GARNISH: FRESHLY GRATED NUTMEG

combine all of the ingredients in a large heated punch bowl (they make these for the classic drink called the Café Brulot). Serve in heated brandy snifters. Garnish each drink with nutmeg.

hot
& STEAMY

All it takes is a few days in a row of below-freezing temperatures, a good snowstorm, or a long afternoon on the slopes to make us crave warm libations, usually served with a kick by way of a spirit. The inspiration for most drinks served steaming goes back to the toddies, used by past generations as old-fashioned cold remedies. Hot toddies are simply mixtures of hot water, sugar, or honey, and a single spirit—usually bourbon. But any whiskey, aged rum, or brandy could be used. Although it was long ago thought that it was the spirit that made you feel better, it was more likely the heat combined with the spirit that did the trick. Either way, you don't have to feel ill to enjoy these drinks, as long as you remember that too much of any good thing can make you feel less than great.

blue blazer

2½ OZ. BLENDED SCOTCH WHISKY

2½ OZ. BOILING WATER

1 TSP. SUGAR

GARNISH: LEMON TWIST

using two large silver-plated or heavy ceramic mugs with handles, put the whisky in one mug and the boiling water in the other. Ignite the whisky carefully with a long match or lighter-wand by touching the surface with the flame. While it is flaming, mix the ingredients by pouring them four or five times from one mug to the other. If done well, this will have the appearance of a continuous stream of liquid fire. Sweeten with the sugar and pour into in a preheated 5-oz. Irish coffee glass. Garnish with the lemon twist.

café l'orange

1 OZ. COGNAC

1 OZ. MANDARINE NAPOLÉON

4 OZ. FRESHLY BREWED COFFEE

FRESHLY WHIPPED CREAM (SEE PAGE 60)

GARNISH: FINELY GRATED ORANGE ZEST

combine the cognac and liqueur in a preheated Irish coffee glass. Add the coffee and stir. Top with a dollop of whipped cream and garnish with a pinch of orange zest.

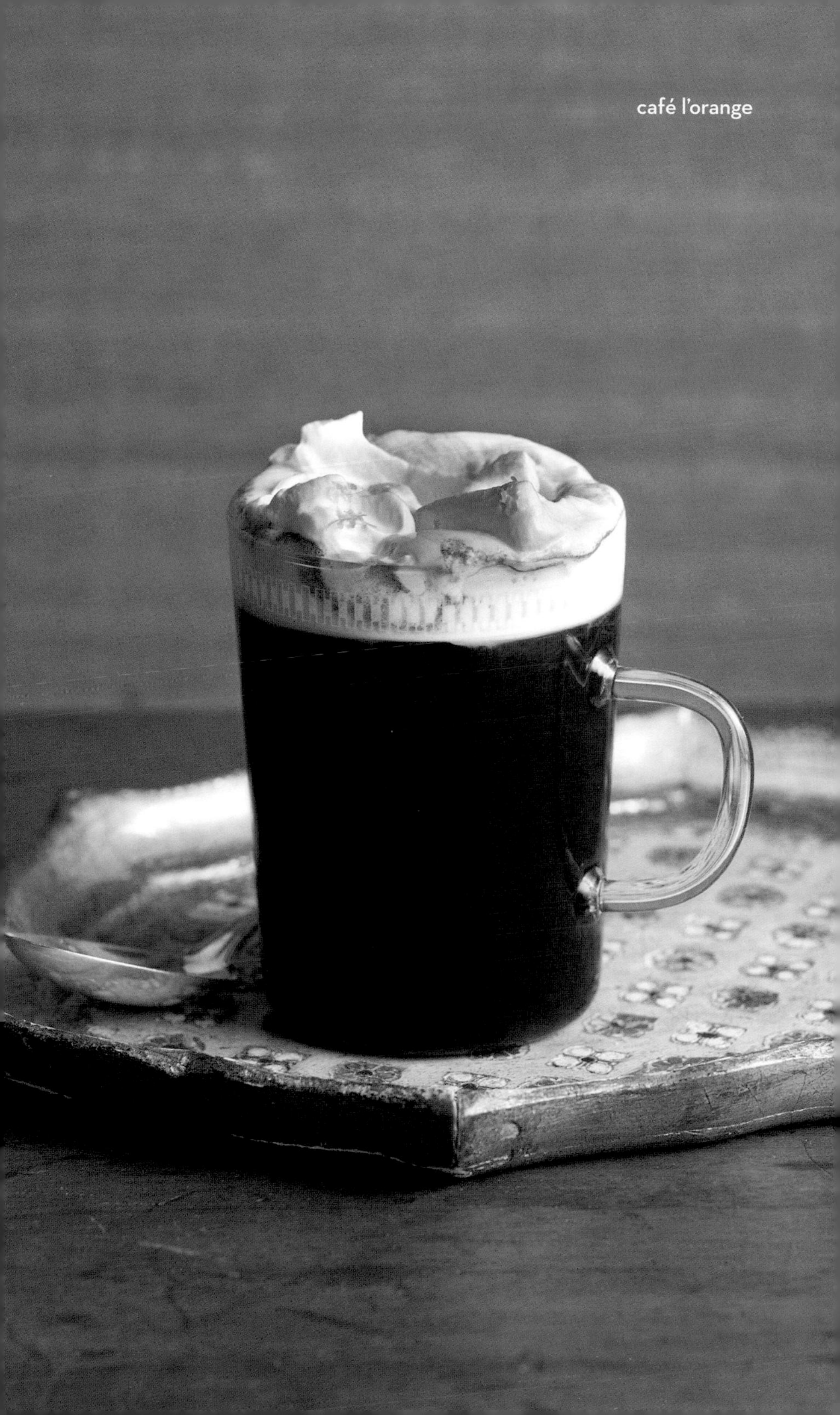

café l'orange

café pacifico

1½ OZ. BLANCO TEQUILA

½ OZ. COFFEE LIQUEUR

4 OZ. FRESHLY BREWED COFFEE

½ TSP. GROUND CINNAMON

1 TSP. SUPERFINE SUGAR, PLUS MORE FOR GARNISH

FRESHLY WHIPPED CREAM (SEE PAGE 60)

GARNISH: CINNAMON STICK

combine the tequila, coffee liqueur, and coffee in a preheated Irish coffee glass. Stir in the cinnamon and sugar. Top with a dollop of whipped cream and garnish with a pinch of sugar and a cinnamon stick.

{trade secret}

A WATCHED POT . . .

For best results in drinks that require tea or coffee, heat the water on your stove and steep in a French press. Coffee should be steeped in water close to 200°F, and tea should be steeped in water ranging from 212°F (boiling) for black teas all the way down to 150°F for green teas. If you don't have a thermometer handy, you can tell the water temperature by watching the bubbles: Small bubbles will float to the surface of the water at 160° to 170°F, and you'll see strings of bubbles from the bottom of the pot at 180° to 190°F.

coffee nudge

½ OZ. BRANDY

½ OZ. COFFEE LIQUEUR

½ OZ. DARK CRÈME DE CACAO

5 OZ. FRESHLY BREWED COFFEE

FRESHLY WHIPPED CREAM (SEE PAGE 60)

GARNISH: GRATED CHOCOLATE

combine the brandy, coffee liqueur, and crème de cacao in a preheated Irish coffee glass. Add the coffee and stir. Top with a dollop of whipped cream and garnish with grated chocolate.

corryvreckan

1 OZ. SINGLE MALT SCOTCH WHISKY

¾ OZ. DRAMBUIE

¼ OZ. GALLIANO

2 OZ. STEAMED MILK

combine all of the ingredients in a preheated Irish coffee glass. Stir and serve immediately.

duckboot

1 OZ. AQUAVIT

1 OZ. MEZCAL DE OAXACA

6 OZ. MEXICAN HOT CHOCOLATE

2 DASHES OF HOT SAUCE

combine all of the ingredients in a preheated Irish coffee glass. Stir and serve immediately.

ginger mac

1½ OZ. TAWNY PORT

3 WHOLE CLOVES

1 TSP. GINGER PRESERVES

1 OZ. SINGLE MALT SCOTCH WHISKY

½ OZ. ORANGE CURAÇAO

GARNISH: ORANGE TWIST

combine the port with the cloves and ginger preserves in a saucepan and heat over a low flame (do not let it come to a boil). Add the Scotch and curaçao and heat thoroughly. Pour into a preheated brandy snifter through a fine-mesh strainer (to remove the pulp and cloves). Garnish with the orange twist.

ginger mac

ginseng toddy

1½ OZ. COGNAC

¾ OZ. HONEY SYRUP (SEE PAGE 3)

½ OZ. FRESH LEMON JUICE

4 OZ. HOT BREWED GINSENG-FLAVORED GREEN TEA

GARNISH: CINNAMON STICK

combine all of the ingredients in a preheated Irish coffee glass and stir. Garnish with the cinnamon stick.

hermit's cloak

1½ OZ. AGED RUM

¾ OZ. BÉNÉDICTINE

5 OZ. MEXICAN HOT CHOCOLATE

GARNISH: LARGE MARSHMALLOW

combine all of the ingredients in a preheated Irish coffee glass and stir. Garnish with the marshmallow.

hot brick toddy

1 TSP. MELTED UNSALTED BUTTER

1 TSP. CONFECTIONERS' SUGAR

3 PINCHES GROUND CINNAMON

1 OZ. IRISH WHISKEY

BOILING WATER (AT LEAST 6 OZ.)

combine the butter, sugar, and cinnamon in a mug and allow the sugar to dissolve thoroughly. Add the whiskey and fill the mug with boiling water. Stir and serve immediately.

{trade secret}

HANDLING HOT DRINKS

Make sure the glassware you're serving your hot drinks in is both tempered (so it doesn't crack when you pour boiling hot liquid into it) and either insulated (so you can hold it without burning your hand) or with a handle. Bodum makes very cool modern insulated glassware that is much easier to handle than those antique tea cups you use alongside cucumber sandwiches. Rinsing each cup or glass with a few ounces of boiling water before serving a hot drink will delay cooling, as well as prepare the cup.

hot buttered rum

hot buttered rum

1 TSP. LIGHT BROWN SUGAR

BOILING WATER

1 TBSP. UNSALTED BUTTER

2 OZ. AGED RUM

GARNISH: FRESHLY GRATED NUTMEG

put the sugar in a mug and fill two-thirds full with boiling water. Add the butter and rum and stir thoroughly. Garnish with nutmeg.

hot mint toddy

3 OZ. HOT WATER

3 FRESH MINT LEAVES

1³/₄ OZ. BOURBON WHISKEY

1 DASH OF ANGOSTURA BITTERS

¹/₂ TSP. MAPLE SYRUP

combine the hot water and mint leaves in a preheated Irish coffee glass. Let steep for about 30 seconds and then strain out the mint leaves. Stir in the bourbon, bitters, and maple syrup and serve immediately.

irish coffee

1½ OZ. IRISH WHISKEY

½ OZ. SIMPLE SYRUP OR 1½ TSP. SUGAR, OR TO TASTE

HOT FRESHLY BREWED COFFEE

FRESHLY WHIPPED CREAM (SEE PAGE 60)

pour the whiskey into a preheated Irish coffee glass. Add the simple syrup and fill to within ½ inch of the top with coffee. Top with a dollop of whipped cream to the brim.

le père bis

1½ OZ. SMOKY SINGLE MALT SCOTCH WHISKY

½ OZ. ELDERFLOWER LIQUEUR

½ OZ. HONEY

4 OZ. HOT BREWED CHAMOMILE TEA

GARNISH: LEMON WEDGE STUDDED WITH WHOLE CLOVES

combine all of the ingredients in a preheated Irish coffee glass and stir. Garnish with the clove-studded lemon wedge.

pumpkin steamer

pumpkin steamer

1 OZ. CANNED PURE PUMPKIN PURÉE

2 OZ. WHOLE MILK

¼ OZ. RICH SIMPLE SYRUP (SEE PAGE 3)

1 OZ. AGED RUM

1 OZ. GALLIANO

2 DASHES OF ANGOSTURA BITTERS

GARNISH: FRESHLY GRATED NUTMEG

combine the pumpkin purée, milk, and syrup in a saucepan and heat until hot but not boiling. Combine the spirits and bitters in a preheated snifter and add the hot mixture. Garnish with nutmeg.

"que calor!"

1/2 OZ. SIMPLE SYRUP

3/4 OZ. FRESH LEMON JUICE

5 OZ. APPLE CIDER

1 1/2 OZ. CACHAÇA

1/4 OZ. ALLSPICE LIQUEUR (ALSO KNOWN AS PIMENTO DRAM)

GARNISH: ORANGE TWIST

combine the simple syrup, lemon juice, and cider in a saucepan and heat until hot but not boiling. Combine the cachaça and allspice liqueur in a preheated Irish coffee glass and add the hot cider. Garnish with the orange twist.

the rose bush

1 1/2 OZ. IRISH WHISKEY

1/2 OZ. ROSE SYRUP

3 OZ. HOT BREWED ENGLISH BREAKFAST TEA

GARNISH: ORANGE TWIST

combine all of the ingredients in a preheated Irish coffee glass and stir. Garnish with the orange twist.

the thomas tribute

Serves 8

12 LARGE EGGS, SEPARATED

4 TSP. GROUND CINNAMON

2 TSP. GROUND CLOVES

2 TSP. GROUND ALLSPICE

2 TSP. CREAM OF TARTAR

4 TBSP. SUGAR

8 OZ. BRANDY

8 OZ. RUM

BOILING WATER

GARNISH: FRESHLY GRATED NUTMEG

beat the egg whites to stiff peaks. Separately, beat the yolks until combined. Fold the yolks into the whites and add the spices, cream of tartar, and sugar and stir until the egg mixture reaches the consistency of a light batter. For each drink, combine 1 tbsp. of the egg mixture, 2 oz. brandy, and 2 oz. of rum in a preheated Irish coffee glass and fill the glass with boiling water. Garnish with nutmeg.

uva fresca

1 1/2 OZ. BLANCO TEQUILA
1/2 OZ. GREEN CHARTREUSE
1/2 OZ. CONCORD GRAPE JUICE
3 OZ. HOT BREWED HIBISCUS TEA
GARNISH: LIME TWIST

combine all of the ingredients in a preheated Irish coffee glass. Garnish with the lime twist.

uva fresca

verte chaud

2 OZ. GREEN CHARTREUSE

6 OZ. HOT CHOCOLATE

FRESHLY WHIPPED CREAM (SEE BELOW)

combine the Chartreuse and hot chocolate in a preheated Irish coffee glass and stir. Top with a dollop of whipped cream.

{trade secret}

COOL WHIPPED

Resist the urge to buy ready-whipped cream; it's usually sweetened and lacks the texture of freshly whipped cream that can be spooned on top of a hot drink. All it takes is fresh heavy cream and a minute or two with a handheld mixer to whip up the perfect topping—though hats off to those who whisk by hand! This luxurious spread can then be sprinkled with freshly grated nutmeg or other ground baking spices to lure your guests closer to the glass.

rich
& CREAMY

There's a very good as well as perfectly logical reason why a piping hot bowl of beef stew, a cassoulet, or slow-braised short ribs seem to taste better in the winter months than when it's warmer: Our bodies' tastes and cravings change with the seasons. And just as rib-stickingly satisfying foods tend to fortify and warm us up, so too do rich, creamy cocktails made with silky, viscous ingredients like eggs and cream. This notion, of course, is not new. According to the *Oxford English Dictionary*, the very first egg-based drinks, known as *flips*, appeared in the late 1600s and were described as amalgams of beer, rum, sugar, and eggs, heated with a red-hot iron that caused the drink to froth (or flip). Three centuries later the flip has evolved into a cold cocktail consisting of spirit, egg, sugar, and spice, while its close cousin, the nog, is basically a flip with the addition of cream. (For concerns about using eggs, please refer to page vii of the Introduction and "Employing Eggs" on page 75.)

abbotts and friars

½ OZ. BÉNÉDICTINE

1 OZ. SLOE GIN

8 OZ. ABBEY ALE

combine all of the ingredients in a brandy snifter, stir, and serve.

añogo

1½ OZ. AÑEJO TEQUILA

1 OZ. WHOLE MILK

¾ OZ. AGAVE NECTAR

¼ OZ. VANILLA EXTRACT

1 WHOLE EGG

GARNISHES: FRESHLY GRATED NUTMEG; FLAMED ORANGE TWIST

combine all of the ingredients in a mixing glass and shake without ice. Add ice cubes, shake, and strain into a chilled highball glass. Garnish with nutmeg and the flamed orange twist.

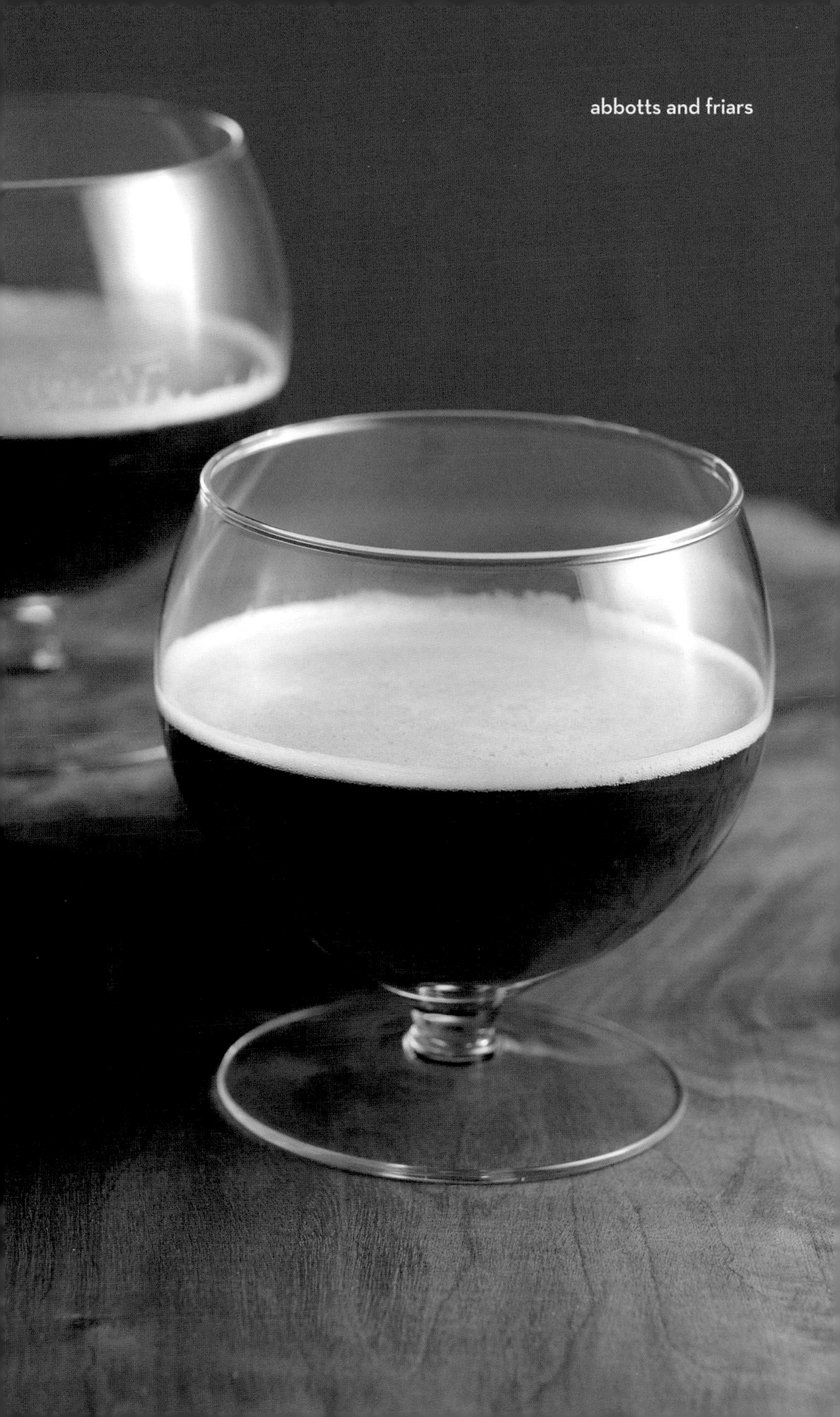
abbotts and friars

banane flip

banane flip

4 VANILLA WAFER COOKIES, PLUS 1 FOR GARNISH

3 OZ. BOURBON WHISKEY

3/4 OZ. CRÈME DE BANANE

1/2 OZ. SIMPLE SYRUP

1 LARGE EGG

GARNISH: THIN BANANA SLICE

muddle the vanilla wafers into a paste in a mixing glass or cocktail shaker. Add the rest of the ingredients and shake without ice. Add ice cubes, shake, and strain into a fizz or old-fashioned glass. Garnish with a cookie and the banana slice.

brunswick street cocktail

1 1/2 OZ. COGNAC

1 1/2 OZ. SHERRY (PEDRO XIMENEZ)

1 LARGE EGG YOLK

GARNISH: FRESHLY GRATED NUTMEG

combine all of the ingredients in a cocktail shaker filled with ice cubes and shake thoroughly. Strain into a chilled cocktail glass. Garnish with nutmeg.

chi-town flip

2 OZ. BOURBON WHISKEY

3/4 OZ. TAWNY PORT

3/4 OZ. FRESH LEMON JUICE

3/4 OZ. LICOR 43

1/4 OZ. SIMPLE SYRUP

1 LARGE EGG

GARNISHES: FRESHLY GRATED NUTMEG; ANGOSTURA BITTERS

combine all of the ingredients in a cocktail shaker and shake without ice. Add ice cubes, shake, and strain into a Collins glass. Garnish with nutmeg and three drops of Angostura bitters.

the corenwyn alexander

1 OZ. BOLS CORENWYN (GENEVER)

1 OZ. DARK CRÈME DE CACAO

1 1/2 OZ. WHOLE MILK

1/2 OZ. RICH SIMPLE SYRUP (SEE PAGE 3)

GARNISH: GRATED DARK CHOCOLATE

combine all of the ingredients in a cocktail shaker and add ice cubes. Shake thoroughly and strain into a chilled Champagne coupe. Garnish with grated chocolate.

the corenwyn alexander

divisadero punch

1 OZ. CALVADOS

1 OZ. AÑEJO TEQUILA

½ OZ. RICH SIMPLE SYRUP (SEE PAGE 3)

2 OZ. WHOLE MILK

2 DASHES OF ANGOSTURA BITTERS

GARNISH: ORANGE TWIST STUDDED WITH WHOLE CLOVES

combine all of the ingredients in a cocktail shaker and add ice cubes. Shake thoroughly and strain into a old-fashioned glass filled with ice cubes. Garnish with the orange twist.

dufftown flip

2 OZ. SINGLE MALT SCOTCH WHISKY

½ OZ. RUBY PORT

½ OZ. SIMPLE SYRUP

¾ OZ. ALMOND MILK

1 LARGE EGG

GARNISH: FRESHLY GRATED NUTMEG

combine all of the ingredients in a cocktail shaker and shake for 10 seconds. Add ice cubes, shake thoroughly, and strain into a chilled snifter. Garnish with nutmeg.

eggnog (homemade)

Serves 8

6 LARGE EGGS

1 CUP SUGAR

12 OZ. AGED RUM

16 OZ. HALF-AND-HALF

16 OZ. WHOLE MILK

GARNISH: FRESHLY GRATED NUTMEG

beat the eggs in a large bowl until foamy. Add the sugar and beat until the batter becomes thick and lemon-colored. Stir in the rest of the ingredients. Chill for at least 3 hours. Garnish with nutmeg.

fiametta

1¹/₂ OZ. WHITE RUM

1 OZ. HALF-AND-HALF

¹/₂ OZ. FRESH LIME JUICE

2 TSP. ORGEAT

1 TSP. CRÈME DE PÊCHE

1 OZ. SODA WATER

¹/₂ OZ. RUBY PORT

combine the first five ingredients in a cocktail shaker and add ice cubes. Shake thoroughly and strain into a chilled highball glass. Top off with the soda water and carefully float the port on top.

frostbite

2 OZ. BLANCO TEQUILA

¾ OZ. WHITE CRÈME DE CACAO

¾ OZ. HEAVY CREAM

GARNISH: FRESHLY GRATED NUTMEG

combine all of the ingredients in a cocktail shaker and add ice cubes. Shake thoroughly and strain into a chilled cocktail glass. Garnish with nutmeg.

gran café arroz

1½ OZ. REPOSADO TEQUILA
½ OZ. COFFEE LIQUEUR
2 OZ. HORCHATA (CINNAMON-FLAVORED RICE MILK)
GARNISH: GROUND CINNAMON

combine all of the ingredients in a cocktail shaker and add ice cubes. Shake thoroughly and strain into a old-fashioned glass filled with ice cubes. Garnish with ground cinnamon.

great pumpkin

2 OZ. PUMPKIN-FLAVORED BEER
1 OZ. STRAIGHT RYE WHISKEY
1 OZ. APPLE BRANDY
½ OZ. GRADE B MAPLE SYRUP
1 LARGE EGG
GARNISH: FRESHLY GRATED NUTMEG

pour the beer into a mixing glass 20 minutes before serving to decarbonate. Add the rest of the ingredients to the mixing glass and shake without ice. Add ice cubes, shake, and strain into a fizz or old-fashioned glass. Garnish with nutmeg.

jerez flip

1 OZ. PEDRO XIMENEZ SHERRY
1 OZ. CREAM SHERRY
3/4 OZ. FRESH ORANGE JUICE
1 LARGE EGG
1 OZ. HEAVY CREAM
1/2 OZ. SIMPLE SYRUP
GARNISH: ORANGE TWIST

combine all of the ingredients in a cocktail shaker and shake without ice. Add ice cubes, shake thoroughly, and strain into a chilled Champagne coupe. Garnish with the orange twist.

new york flip

2 OZ. STRAIGHT RYE WHISKEY
3/4 OZ. RUBY PORT
3/4 OZ. SIMPLE SYRUP
1 OZ. HEAVY CREAM
1 LARGE EGG
GARNISH: FRESHLY GRATED NUTMEG

combine all of the ingredients in a cocktail shaker and shake without ice. Add ice cubes, shake thoroughly, and strain into a chilled Champagne flute. Garnish with nutmeg.

pit stop flip

1½ OZ. APPLE BRANDY

½ OZ. RAINWATER MADEIRA

½ OZ. MAPLE SYRUP

½ OZ. HEAVY CREAM

1 LARGE EGG YOLK

GARNISH: FRESHLY GRATED NUTMEG

combine all of the ingredients in a cocktail shaker and shake without ice. Add ice cubes, shake, and strain into a chilled fizz or highball glass. Garnish with nutmeg.

px flip

1½ OZ. BLANCO TEQUILA

¾ OZ. PEDRO XIMENEZ SHERRY

½ OZ. HEAVY CREAM

½ OZ. SIMPLE SYRUP

1 EGG

1 DASH ORANGE BITTERS

1 DASH ORANGE FLOWER WATER

combine all of the ingredients in a cocktail shaker and shake without ice. Add ice cubes, shake, and strain into a Collins glass.

savory barbados flip

5 FRESH SAGE LEAVES, PLUS 1 FOR GARNISH

1 OZ. COCONUT MILK

1½ OZ. AGED RUM

1 OZ. HAZELNUT LIQUEUR

1 LARGE EGG

GARNISHES: FRESHLY GRATED NUTMEG; GROUND CINNAMON

muddle the sage leaves with the coconut milk in a mixing glass or cocktail shaker. Add the rest of the ingredients and shake without ice. Add ice cubes, shake, and strain into a chilled Champagne coupe. Garnish with a sage leaf, nutmeg, and cinnamon.

{trade secret}

EMPLOYING EGGS

Experts estimate the risk of salmonella contamination from raw eggs to be about 1 in 20,000. That means you're more likely to drown. If those odds are too steep, pasteurized eggs can be used in drinks that require egg yolks, like flips and nogs.

In general, the fresher the egg, the better the texture and flavor you will attain in your drink. Look for large organic eggs, and remember to mix the drink in the mixing glass and crack the egg into the metal half of the Boston shaker: that way, if you botch the egg-breaking operation, you can dump it out and do it over without wasting any precious liquor.

Lastly, to fully emulsify a shaken drink made with egg whites or yolks, shake the drink without ice for 10 seconds, then add ice and shake again to mix and chill.

sleepy hollow fizz

1¹/₂ OZ. AGED RUM
¹/₂ OZ. OVERPROOF DARK RUM
¹/₂ OZ. FRESH LEMON JUICE
¹/₂ OZ. MAPLE SYRUP
1 TSP. CANNED PURE PUMPKIN PURÉE
1 LARGE EGG YOLK
SODA WATER

combine all of the ingredients in a cocktail shaker and shake without ice. Add ice cubes, shake, and strain into a fizz or old-fashioned glass. Top with a splash of soda water.

snowball

1¹/₂ OZ. GIN
¹/₂ OZ. ANISETTE
¹/₂ OZ. HEAVY CREAM

combine all of the ingredients in a cocktail shaker and add ice cubes. Shake thoroughly and strain into a chilled cocktail glass.

sleepy hollow fizz

wallbanger flip

wallbanger flip

2 OZ. VODKA

1 OZ. FRESH ORANGE JUICE

½ OZ. GALLIANO

1 LARGE EGG

3 DASHES OF PEYCHAUD'S BITTERS

combine all of the ingredients in a cocktail shaker and shake without ice. Add ice cubes, shake thoroughly, and strain into a chilled cocktail glass.

{trade secret}

GRENADINE GRIT

True grenadine syrup made with fresh pomegranate juice is exponentially better than anything you can buy already prepared—in fact, given all the additives and food coloring used to concoct most commercial brands, they shouldn't even be allowed to bear the name grenadine. While using fresh pomegranate seeds is the truest way to make this, thanks to the availability of pomegranate juice in fine markets (such as POM Wonderful), you can make this pretty easily.

combine equal parts sugar and pomegranate juice in a saucepan. Heat to dissolve. Simmer until the liquid is thick enough to stick to the back of a metal spoon, about 15 minutes. Remove from the heat, add 3 drops of orange flower water per cup of syrup, and refrigerate to cool. Store in the refrigerator.

highly SPIRITED

With the holidays come days that grow colder and grayer, as well as darker more quickly. Whether it's psychological or practical, it seems like we tend to gravitate toward darker spirits, perhaps to suit that mood. Darker spirits almost always possess deeper flavor and complexity and, often coupled with higher alcohol, give the perception of warmth and satiety. When it's dark before 5:00 pm, it doesn't feel too soon to be enjoying a cocktail during the late afternoon, while in the summer months, it would probably feel preposterously early. And just as we expect more heft and comfort in our wintry foods, so too do we crave more depth and body in the drinks we imbibe. So to that end, we propose these highly spirited drinks for comforting contemplation by the fire, festive holiday parties, and everything in between.

autumn leaves

autumn leaves

¾ OZ. STRAIGHT RYE WHISKEY

¾ OZ. APPLE BRANDY

¾ OZ. SWEET VERMOUTH

¼ OZ. STREGA

2 DASHES OF ANGOSTURA BITTERS

GARNISH: ORANGE TWIST

combine all of the ingredients in a mixing glass. Add ice cubes, stir, and strain into an old-fashioned glass filled with ice cubes. Garnish with the orange twist.

autumn vitae

1 OZ. AQUAVIT

¾ OZ. APPLE BRANDY

¾ OZ. SWEET VERMOUTH

¼ OZ. YELLOW CHARTREUSE

1 DASH OF ANGOSTURA BITTERS

GARNISH: LEMON TWIST

combine all of the ingredients in a mixing glass. Add ice cubes, stir, and strain into a chilled Champagne coupe. Garnish with the lemon twist.

bijou cocktail

1 OZ. GIN

1 OZ. GREEN CHARTREUSE

1 OZ. SWEET VERMOUTH

1 DASH OF ORANGE BITTERS

combine all of the ingredients in a mixing glass. Add ice cubes, stir, and strain into a chilled cocktail glass.

chancellor cocktail

2 OZ. SCOTCH WHISKY

³/₄ OZ. DRY VERMOUTH

³/₄ OZ. RUBY PORT

1 DASH OF PEYCHAUD'S BITTERS

GARNISH: LEMON TWIST

combine all of the ingredients in a mixing glass. Add ice cubes, stir, and strain into a chilled cocktail glass. Garnish with the lemon twist.

bijou cocktail

dreamy dorini
smoking martini

clove

2 OZ. VODKA

½ OZ. DRY VERMOUTH

2 DASHES OF ORANGE BITTERS

GARNISH: ORANGE TWIST STUDDED WITH 1 CLOVE

combine all of the ingredients in a mixing glass. Add ice cubes, stir, and strain into a chilled Champagne coupe. Garnish with the orange twist.

dreamy dorini smoking martini

2 OZ. VODKA

½ OZ. SMOKY SINGLE MALT SCOTCH WHISKY

4 DROPS OF PASTIS

GARNISH: LEMON TWIST

combine all of the ingredients in a mixing glass. Add ice cubes, stir, and strain into a chilled cocktail glass. Garnish with the lemon twist.

green glacier

2 OZ. COGNAC

¾ OZ. GREEN CHARTREUSE

¼ OZ. WHITE CRÈME DE CACAO

2 DASHES OF ANGOSTURA BITTERS

combine all of the ingredients in a mixing glass. Add ice cubes, stir, and strain into a chilled Champagne coupe.

green glacier

high plains drifter no. 2

2 OZ. REPOSADO TEQUILA

¾ OZ. SWEET VERMOUTH

½ OZ. GREEN CHARTREUSE

1 DASH OF ORANGE BITTERS

CAMPARI

GARNISH: ORANGE TWIST

combine the first four ingredients in a mixing glass. Add ice cubes, stir, and strain into a chilled Campari-rinsed Champagne coupe. Garnish with the orange twist.

jack maples

2 OZ. APPLEJACK

½ TSP. MAPLE SYRUP

1 DASH OF FEE'S AROMATIC BITTERS

GARNISH: CINNAMON STICK

combine all of the ingredients in a mixing glass. Add ice cubes, stir, and strain into a chilled cocktail glass. Garnish with the cinnamon stick.

jerry's medicine

2¹/₂ OZ. AGED RUM

¹/₂ OZ. PEDRO XIMENEZ SHERRY

¹/₄ OZ. CRÈME DE BANANE

2 DASHES OF ANGOSTURA BITTERS

4 DASHES OF ORANGE BITTERS

GARNISH: FLAMED ORANGE TWIST (SEE BELOW)

combine all of the ingredients in a mixing glass. Add ice cubes, stir, and strain into a chilled old-fashioned glass with 1 large ice cube. Garnish with the flamed orange twist.

{trade secret}

CONSERVE OIL

For drinks garnished with a citrus twist, be sure to cut or twist the peel over the surface of the drink so you don't lose all of the aromatic oils spraying out. The best way is to cut a quarter-sized disk of peel and pinch it, skin side out, between your thumb, index, and middle finger over the glass. For a twist over your brown-spirit drinks, try flaming: Hold a lit match between the surface of the drink and the disk and ignite the aromatic oils. Just be sure not to let the tip of the match touch the twist.

joan crawford

2 OZ. GIN
3/4 OZ. DRY VERMOUTH
1/2 OZ. STREGA
GARNISH: GRAPEFRUIT TWIST

combine all of the ingredients in a mixing glass. Add ice cubes, stir, and strain into a chilled Champagne coupe. Garnish with the grapefruit twist.

la perla

1 1/2 OZ. REPOSADO TEQUILA
1 1/2 OZ. MANZANILLA SHERRY
3/4 OZ. PEAR LIQUEUR
GARNISH: LEMON TWIST

combine all of the ingredients in a mixing glass. Add ice cubes, stir, and strain into a chilled cocktail glass. Garnish with the lemon twist.

the oaxaca
old fashioned

1½ OZ. REPOSADO TEQUILA

½ OZ. MEZCAL DE OAXACA

¼ OZ. AGAVE NECTAR

2 DASHES OF ANGOSTURA BITTERS

GARNISH: ORANGE TWIST

combine all of the ingredients in a mixing glass. Add ice cubes, stir, and strain into a chilled old-fashioned glass. Garnish with the orange twist.

occidental

2 OZ. LINIE AQUAVIT

¾ OZ. GRAND MARNIER

½ OZ. AMARO

FERNET-BRANCA

GARNISH: ORANGE TWIST

combine the first three ingredients in a mixing glass. Add ice cubes, stir, and strain into a chilled, Fernet-Branca–rinsed Champagne coupe. Garnish with the orange twist.

the revolver

2 OZ. BOURBON WHISKEY

½ OZ. COFFEE LIQUEUR

2 DASHES OF ORANGE BITTERS

GARNISH: FLAMED ORANGE TWIST (SEE PAGE 91)

combine all of the ingredients in a mixing glass. Add ice cubes, stir, and strain into a chilled Champagne coupe. Garnish with the flamed orange twist.

the sherry-netherland

12 RAISINS, PLUS 3 FOR GARNISH

2 OZ. GENEVER

1 OZ. PEDRO XIMENEZ SHERRY

¼ OZ. ORANGE CURAÇAO

2 DASHES OF ORANGE BITTERS

muddle the raisins in a mixing glass. Add the rest of the ingredients. Add ice cubes, stir, and strain through a tea strainer into a chilled Champagne coupe. Garnish with 3 raisins on a pick.

virginia dare

virginia dare

1 PEAR SLICE, PLUS 1 FOR GARNISH

2 OZ. AGED RUM

½ OZ. BÉNÉDICTINE

2 DASHES OF ANGOSTURA BITTERS

muddle 1 pear slice in a mixing glass. Add the rest of the ingredients. Stir with ice cubes and strain through a fine-mesh sieve into a chilled cocktail glass. Garnish with the remaining pear slice.

v.p.

2¹/₂ OZ. AGED RUM

1 OZ. TAWNY PORT

¹/₂ OZ. SWEET VERMOUTH

¹/₂ OZ. SIMPLE SYRUP

1 DASH OF ANGOSTURA BITTERS

1 DASH OF ORANGE BITTERS

GARNISH: LEMON TWIST

combine all of the ingredients in a mixing glass. Add ice cubes, stir, and strain into a chilled Champagne coupe. Garnish with the lemon twist.

widow's kiss

2 OZ. CALVADOS OR APPLE BRANDY

³/₄ OZ. YELLOW CHARTREUSE

³/₄ OZ. BÉNÉDICTINE

1 DASH OF ANGOSTURA BITTERS

combine all of the ingredients in a mixing glass. Add ice cubes, stir, and strain into a chilled cocktail glass.

the winter waltz

1 OZ. COGNAC

1 OZ. APPLE BRANDY

3/4 OZ. AMARO

1/2 OZ. ALLSPICE LIQUEUR (ALSO KNOWN AS PIMENTO DRAM)

GARNISH: WHOLE STAR ANISE POD

combine all of the ingredients in a mixing glass. Add ice cubes, stir, and strain into a chilled Champagne coupe. Garnish with the star anise.

MEASURE BY MEASURE

Measure your drinks into a mixing glass to ensure consistency, as well as to see what you're doing. It's best to mix all of the ingredients together before adding the ice. Store your mixing glass with your glassware in the freezer if you have room, but keep your spirits on the shelf—you won't achieve proper dilution if you store everything in the freezer.

measures

Here are conversions for unusual measures typically found in nineteenth-century recipes:

Pony/Cordial = 1 ounce

Pousse Café Glass = 1.5 ounces

Cocktail Glass = 2 ounces

Gill = 4 ounces

Wine Glass = 4 ounces

Small Tumbler = 8 ounces

Large Tumbler = 16 ounces

STANDARD BAR MEASUREMENTS (U.S.)

Pony = 1 ounce

1 ounce = 3 centiliters

Jigger, shot = 1.5 ounces

Mixing Glass = 16 ounces

Splash = ½ ounce

6 drops = 2 dashes = ⅙ teaspoon

OTHER MEASURES

3 drops = 1 dash

12 dashes = 1 teaspoon

1 teaspoon = ⅛ ounce

2 teaspoons = ¼ ounce

1 tablespoon = ½ ounce

2 tablespoons = 1 ounce

¼ cup = 2 ounces

½ cup = 4 ounces

1 cup or ½ pint = 8 ounces

2 cups or 1 pint = 16 ounces

4 cups, 2 pints, or 1 quart = 32 ounces

BOTTLE SIZE MEASURES

Split = 187 ml = 6.4 ounces

Half-Bottle = 375 ml = 12.7 ounces

Fifth = 750 ml = 25.4 ounces

Liter = 1000 ml = 33.8 ounces

Magnum = 1.5 liters = 2 wine bottles

Jeroboam = 3 liters = 4 wine bottles

Rehoboam = 6 wine bottles

Methuselah = 8 wine bottles

Salmanazar = 12 wine bottles

Balthazar = 16 wine bottles

Nebuchadnezzar = 20 wine bottles

Sovereign = 34 wine bottles

INDEX